Angel

Country

Angelic Encounters:
True Stories from Maine

Ria Biley

Walk with Angels!

Ria Biley

Published by Angelis Press
Rockland, Maine

Published by Angelis Press
Rockland, Maine

First Edition, October 1995

Second Printing, January 1996

Production design & typesetting by Ria Biley

Cover illustration by Glen Birbeck

Library of Congress Catalog Card No: 95-95050

ISBN: 1-57502-067-X

Printed in the USA by

*M*ᴑ**RRIS**
PUBLISHING

3212 E. Hwy 30
Kearney, NE 68847
800-650-7888

ෆ◆ෆ

For Rose West
whose Angelic qualities
have provided me with
a lifetime of emotional
and spiritual support.

ෆ◆ෆ

Contents

$\mathcal{F}$oreword

The stories in *Angel Country* are all true. The people in *Angel Country* are your neighbors. With one clearly specified exception, all names are real, and only a few stories do not divulge whole names.

These experiences came to me from all over Maine, by letters, FAXes and telephone calls, from ordinary people whose lives have been touched in extraordinary ways. They tell of rescues, healings, voices and visions—miracles large and small, touching all levels of the human condition.

In retelling these stories, I have endeavored to remain true to the events as told to me. As much as possible, I have used direct quotations from the contributors. Any embellishment on my part has been merely to help my readers share the experience more thoroughly by seeing the events more clearly in their minds' eye.

Although not all of the Angelic encounters recounted here took place within Maine's boundaries, they did originate with people who live in Maine now. I believe that they, like me, were drawn here by synchronistic events not entirely in their own control. And they have found contentment and a better life than they had wherever they started out.

Before I came to Maine, I had always been mindful of God in my life. But I don't think I consciously considered myself surrounded by Angels. That all changed when I moved here. I began to feel differently about being alive, in general, and about being in Maine, in particular.

One day, when I was feeling glad to be alive and in Maine, I spontaneously exclaimed to my husband, "Our Angels are happy here!" He agreed with me, and soon it became a daily recitation in our home. It was, I thought, a very logical explanation for the contentment I suddenly felt. I liked the way I felt when I said it, too. I guess the Angels appreciated being acknowledged regularly, because they began to make us even more aware of their presence in our lives every day.

Some of the people in this book who have contributed Angelic experiences also came here "from away". Whatever they thought their reasons were, I think their Angels wanted to be here, where so many of their kind seem to gravitate. I imagine their Angels arranged the synchronistic events of their lives so they could be united with their celestial comrades. Maybe the native Mainers were always aware of them; the Native Americans certainly were. There is much here in Maine to feed the spirit.

I wish to express my deep appreciation to the people of Maine for sharing their very personal Angelic experiences with me, and with you. I offer apologies to the many people whose stories, due to limitation of space, do not appear here. I hope to include those stories in a subsequent book.

&)✦CR

$\mathscr{A}$cknowledgements

I am grateful for the support this project has generated from so many individuals. When people found out I was writing a book about Angelic Encounters in Maine, they all had something encouraging to say, and many offered positive help. I cannot possibly name them all, but I would like to acknowledge a few here:

My sincere thanks go to members of the Maine media, and especially to Susan Farley, Terry Bowman and the news team at WABI-TV (Channel 5 in Bangor). Their quick and enthusiastic response in getting the word out about my book and my request for encounters opened the floodgates of responses from eastern and central Maine.

Here in the midcoast, thanks to Steve Betts and Tom Von Malder for a spectacular half-page article in the *Courier-Gazette*, and to Bruce Carpenter of WKSQ-FM in Ellsworth for getting the most impressive mileage out of a single radio interview I have ever heard. Thanks also go to the *Coastal Journal, Republican Journal* and *Bangor Daily News*. Because of the diversity of responses I received, I know there were others who published my request. Since I was unable to determine the sources in all cases, I offer an all-inclusive "Thank you!" to all those in the Maine media who helped publicize my efforts. Without media support, I would have been hard pressed to find people willing to share such wonderful experiences.

I have to thank my husband, Frank, for the many evenings he spent alone while I remained glued to my computer, and most especially for awakening me to the importance of writing this book.

Thanks to Rockland artist Glen Birbeck, who, while professing ignorance of such things as Angels, managed to quickly grasp the full meaning and spirit of *Angel Country* in creating the cover illustration for this book.

I'd also like to thank Carolyn Philbrook for her invaluable technical assistance, and Woody Richards for his spiritual guidance and encouragement.

Special thanks go to my dear friend, Lucille Sprague Blackler, whose relentless pursuit of perfection qualified her to be the only person I would entrust with the painstaking job of proofreading my manuscript.

Ultimately, I am grateful to God and my Angels who have guided and protected me all my life, and who have inspired every word in this book.

Welcome to *Angel Country*!

ഔ ✦ beta

$\mathcal{I}_s$ $\mathcal{M}aine$ $\mathcal{A}ngel$ $\mathcal{C}ountry?$

O F COURSE IT IS! A more appropriate question might be *Why* is Maine Angel Country?

The Native Americans have long considered what we now call Maine to be "sacred ground". Perhaps it is. Certainly, there is a power here; a positive power that watches over her people and blesses them graciously. Indisputably, the soul of Maine is her people.

In the two years I have lived here, I have found the people of Maine to be very special, very different from people elsewhere in America, and even in the world. Perhaps it's their fierce independence, their tolerance of ideas and people different from themselves, their trusting, open ways with strangers, or their powerful work ethic. Whatever the reason, it's a wonderful difference.

Maine is such a large state, and its tiny population consists largely of families who have lived here for generations. I truly believe the Angelic presence must be concentrated here. It certainly seems that way to me.

Then again, maybe the correct answer is, "All of the above."

People who have never visited Maine have a preconceived notion that New Englanders (and Mainers in particular) are detached and unfriendly. To the contrary, I have discovered the opposite to be true. There is something about living here that makes people respect one another, accept one another, and generally reject pretentiousness.

Whatever makes Mainers what they are, their little corner of the world has become a haven of tranquillity for me. Since I came here to live, I have become more acutely aware of benevolent intervention in my life than I have ever been before. I began to experience a peace and happiness that had escaped me in all my travels and in all my previous endeavors. I have lived all over the country, and never felt "home" until I arrived here. This sense of belonging has wrapped my spirit in warm, cuddly comfort, like flannel sheets from L.L. Bean on a frigid night.

Sometimes, I get the feeling that if I were to leave the state, I might vaporize—just cease to exist, so complete is my joy at living among Maine's people and amidst all this natural beauty. Like a lovesick teenager, I am still in love with Maine. I find new things to appreciate about her every day.

Here, where mountains meet the sea, the air is fragrant with pine and salt spray. The sound of dueling foghorns tenderly soothes me to sleep at night like a misty lullaby. Each season has its special perfumes—the fragrance of August rain, the musky aroma of October's leaves, the brisk promise of snow in December's air, the fresh pines and heady aromatic lilacs in May.

There is a feast for the eyes everywhere you look in Maine: meticulously manicured hayfields as far as the eye can see; dense, lush forests filled with countless colors; stately sea captains' homes and ancient farmhouses; harbors brimming with magnificent schooners from bygone days, moored majestically beside unassuming lobster boats; lighthouses shrouded in fog—and on a winter's dawn, that most ethereal of nature's effects—sea smoke. (I love this place! Can you tell?)

All these details (and more!) contribute to the beauty that surrounds us every day here in Angel Country. I know the Native Americans must have been right about this place— how could the Angels not rejoice at such surroundings here on earth?

It has been said that when you cross the Kittery Bridge into Maine, you should set your watch back twenty-five years. That may seem like a disadvantage to some, but if you long for the days when teenagers were still kids, instead of terrorists with automatic weapons; when neighbors left their houses unlocked and looked out for one another; when Main Street was a hodgepodge of family-owned shops instead of an anonymous highway full of look-alike neon signs hawking identical wares in every city and town on the map; when a 35 mph speed limit was "fast enough"; when the turning of every season was a major event to be celebrated—if your heart and soul are "lost in the fifties"—then turning back your clock twenty-five or thirty years is not such a bad idea. It worked for me.

If the foregoing has inspired any of you folks "from away" to start packing your bags and rushing our borders, let me caution you—*Maine is not for sissies.* It's not for everyone (if it were, then everyone would be here and it would be just like every place else. Well, almost.). One Maine winter (especially one like 1994) can send even the most determined Yuppie scurrying back to warmer climes.

The stories of Maine people and their encounters with Angels here, where life is the way it should be, are what I want to share with you.

$\wp \blacklozenge \wr$

Why I wrote this book

At last count (February, 1995), there were already more than a hundred books either currently in print or about to be published on the subject of Angels (*Books in Print*, R.R. Bowker). Do we really need another one? Of course, my answer has to be yes.

Let me say from the outset that I did not decide to "jump on the bandwagon" because Angels are "hot".

I have been convinced for years that I am under divine protection of the Angelic kind, and I will share in these pages some of the personal experiences that led me to that conviction. But the focus of *Angel Country* is on *the people of Maine* for very specific reasons; mine are but a few of the encounters you will read here.

For some years, I have been a professional writer—producing primarily fundraising and public relations material for business clients. But when it came to writing about something that was personally important to me, I couldn't seem to focus. In order for a writer to be productive, there must be a burning desire to communicate some*thing* to some*one*. Without the inspiration, it is all too easy not to write.

My inspiration finally came by way of a remarkable series of extraordinary events; you could say the writing of this book chose *me*. Could it be my mission to be PR agent for Maine's Angels?

Since I began compiling all the personal experiences that led to my decision to write about Angelic Encounters, I have been, for lack of a better word, possessed. Nothing I have undertaken before has lit such a fire under me, and I don't believe I can be successful at any endeavor until I have fulfilled this mission.

Back to those ever-popular books. Their enduring popularity is an indicator of public interest in these exceptional events. I believe that one reason so many people are reading these Angel books is to reaffirm their own experiences.

Few of us openly share these experiences, afraid of appearing foolish. But there is a measure of comfort in the anonymity of reading someone else's account. It can make us feel less alone; it can, in effect, validate our own faith.

Many of us were brought up to believe in a personal Guardian Angel. Statistics show that large numbers of us still do. Surprisingly, a 1988 Gallup Poll (*Teen Belief in Angels is on the Rise*, Princeton, NJ) concluded that three out of four American teenagers expressed a belief in Angels. We are speaking of a generation of adolescents exposed to drugs, violence, drive-by shootings, pornography, AIDS—all highly negative input, intrusively driven home on a daily basis by media not even invented in their parents' day. Yet, surprisingly, many are able to maintain this youthful ideal. Clearly, such a belief is not something we relinquish with maturity. An even earlier Gallup poll (*A Surprising Number of Americans Believe in Paranormal Phenomena*, Princeton, NJ 1978) indicated that two out of every three adults in America still believe strongly in the existence of Angels. And as recently as December 1993, TIME magazine's poll showed 69% of those asked believe in the existence of Angels; 46% believe they have a personal Guardian Angel, and 32% of the people polled said they had personally felt an Angelic presence in their lives.

As adults, we may have put aside our childhood myths of Santa, the Easter Bunny, and the Tooth Fairy, but Angels don't abandon us when we grow up. Their job is to guide and protect us—sometimes from ourselves.

These are often frightening times. Maybe we hear more about Angels now because we need Angels now, more than ever.

I am no great scholar of the Bible; Billy Graham, however, is. His book, *Angels, God's Secret Agents*, cites nearly three hundred Angelic references in both the Old and New Testaments. It is natural to assume that believers in God must also believe in the existence and protection of His Angels. Judging by the number of times Angels are mentioned in the Bible, it would follow that a denial of their existence would be a fundamental denial of God Himself.

Angels have appeared throughout history to people of all religious and cultural backgrounds. God knows no boundaries, and His love for us is unconditional. Providing Angels to safeguard our physical welfare and enrich our spiritual lives is surely an affirmation of that love.

ℵ ♦ ℛ

An encounter with an Angelic being is a gift from God. Psalm 91:11, 12 tells us:

> *For He will command His Angels concerning you to guard you in all your ways; they will lift you up in their hands; so that you will not strike your foot against a stone.*

It is fitting that having received a gift from God, we should be willing, if not anxious, to give Him credit for it. I personally believe that a fundamental reason we experience such encounters is so that we will, in fact, share them with others.

We can speculate that a few who have received the gift of a supernatural deliverance from impending danger may well have been saved to accomplish some earth-shattering achievement. It is also entirely possible that some have encountered Angels for no other reason than to relate the tale to exactly the person who needs to hear its message of hope.

And that, dear reader, is the purpose of this book: to share with you the message of hope that each Angelic Encounter delivers. That God, however you perceive Him, is interested in you; that He has provided you with celestial Guardians to inspire, guide, comfort and protect you. (And, if you live in Maine, to make you realize how very fortunate you are!)

People I have met casually while I was writing this book often expressed an interest in my project, although, they were sure they had never had such an experience personally. Frequently, during the course of conversation, they would stop me and say, "Now that you mention it...I just remembered something that happened to me... I never told anyone about it...I had totally forgotten all about it until just now!"

I hope the adventures in *Angel Country* awaken in you, too, wonderful memories of a long-forgotten personal encounter with your own Guardian Angel.

℘♦℃

Angels in Your Life

Q. How do Guardian Angels manifest themselves?

A. Any way they want to!

Angels are pure spirit, and therefore exist on a non-physical plane. Often, they perform their Angelic guidance invisibly, so that only the results of that intervention can be observed.

On other occasions, perhaps when they feel that only a physical manifestation will accomplish the task—they can take on human (or animal) form. They can even enlist an unsuspecting passerby to perform their physical tasks for them.

Angels rarely appear in the "classical" (white flowing dress, wings, etc.) form. But when one does, it is because *that is how the Angel wants to be seen*—it knows there will be no mistaking the apparition if it comes in a form the recipient will recognize.

We humans have the tendency to humanize anything be-yond our comprehension—how many times have you seen God depicted as an old man with a beard? God, too, is spirit. Yet in our corporeal state, we need something we can relate to—that is why we refer to God as He, and why we "expect" Angels to appear much as the Renaissance artists depicted them. That is our human mind set. The intellectual capacity of the Angels is such that each per-son's Angel knows instinctively what that person will ac-cept when he or she needs help.

Angels go about their earthly work in a variety of ways; they have infinite imaginations and always seem to know which type of encounter will suit their purpose.

My research has helped me identify several categories of Angelic interventions. For my own convenience, I have grouped them into what I call "degrees" of intervention. And I have attempted to arrange this book along the guidelines of those categories.

ℬ♦ℭ

Degrees of

1st Degree	**Synchronicity**
	Synchronicity has been referred to as "Angels at play".
	When Angels play with us, they communicate by arranging coincidences and auspicious events in our lives which seem to take on meaning beyond the obvious.
	A series of unexplainable coincidences can lead to altered perception or modified behavior, resulting in avoidance of danger or a wonderful opportunity. Incidents of Synchronicity happen so frequently and so subtly, we often do not recognize them as interventions.
2nd Degree	**Invisible Rescue**
	These events are very frequent occurrences in the world of Angelic intervention.
	They have in common a highly unusual set of circumstances with no logical explanation. The person who is the object of the experience "knows" it is impossible, but also knows for certain that it happened.
	An experience of this type can make an otherwise "closed" person open to recognition of further Angelic encounters.
3rd Degree	**Auditory**
	In a 3rd Degree encounter, the person hears an audible voice (or voices) or some other sound, which may alert the individual to danger or a particularly fortuitous opportunity.
	Such encounters should not be confused with the "voices" schizophrenics hear; auditory encounters of the Angelic kind come in the form of a sharp command or warning, and are momentary in nature.

Angelic Encounters

4th Degree	**Apparition**
	A 4th Degree Encounter is marked by the apparition of objects or persons to an individual who is fully awake; often under extreme stress.
	These encounters may also manifest in dreams. A loved one (or even a stranger) offers solutions to a dilemma, warnings of impending danger, opportunity, or comfort.
	Young children are particularly sensitive to Angelic Apparitions, and remember them far into their adulthood. These experiences are "haunting" and not easily forgotten, as if they "want" to be remembered and acted upon.
5th Degree	**Physical Manifestation**
	Angels assume physical forms.
	A stranger appears "out of nowhere" just as you need help; then, just as suddenly, "disappears"– never to be seen again.
	A tap on your shoulder (or a forceful shove!) wakes you out of a sound sleep to warn of a sick child or that your house is on fire.
	These are just a few examples of physical manifestation by Angels.

$\mathcal{B}$*elief* vs. $\mathcal{K}$*nowledge*

I have quoted several polls in which the vast majority of respondents stated that they believe in Angels. But people do not "believe" in Angels any more than they "believe" in God. "Belief " and "Faith" are two concepts we learned as children. We were taught that having "Faith" means that you "Believe" in something you have not seen.

Anyone who has experienced the affirmation of God's unconditional love will tell you that they *know* there is a God; that they *know* they have been touched by an Angel. I am hardly an expert on religion; I am only an expert on my own life. And the people who so generously contributed to this book are experts on their own lives. Some of them are regular churchgoers; many are not. But all of us *know* by the experiences we share here, that God is interested in our welfare; that He answers our prayers, and that He dispatches His Angels with the answers to those prayers.

℘ ♦ ℭ

Q. Why are Angels interested in our lives?
A. Because it's their job!

Among those books currently in print are a number of well-researched studies of Angelology. If you are interested in learning more about the heavenly hierarchy, I encourage you to invest the time. A recommended reading list for Angel study can be found at the end of this book.

Angel Country deals only with the two lowest levels, those Angels who freely pass between the spiritual and physical realms to interact with Humanity. These are the Archangels and the Angels.

I like to refer to them as "Guardian Variety" Angels.

Angels are ubiquitous. You will find references to them everywhere, not just in religious texts. Many prominent personages have made some very profound statements concerning Angels. A few of my favorites are quoted here—you may find them familiar.

෨ ♦ ☙

Every visible thing in this world is put in the charge of an Angel.

St. Augustine, Eight Questions

℘ ✦ ℭ

Though Angels are both the messengers and the message of God, that makes them no easier to receive. For one thing, we almost never recognize them, even when they knock at our door.

F. Forrester Church

℘ ✦ ℭ

Everyone, no matter how humble he may be, has Angels to watch over him. They are heavenly, pure and splendid, and yet they have been given us to keep us company on our way: they have been given the task of keeping careful watch over you...And not only do they want to protect you from the dangers which waylay you throughout your journey; they are actually by your side, helping your soul as you strive to go ever higher in your union with God...

Pope Pius XII

When ye turn to the right, and when ye turn to the left, thine ears shall hear a voice behind thee, saying, "This is the way; walk ye in it."

Isaiah 30:21

ℰᴑ✦ᴑℛ

The Angel that presided o'er my birth, said, "Little creature formed of Joy & Mirth, go and love without the help of anything on earth."

William Blake

ℰᴑ✦ᴑℛ

Behold, I send an Angel before thee, to keep thee in the way.

Exodus 23:20

ℰᴑ✦ᴑℛ

Round us, too, shall angels shine, such as ministered to thee.

George Hunt Smytten

ℰᴑ✦ᴑℛ

Outside the open window The morning air is all awash with angels.

Richard Wilbur

Silently one by one, in the infinite
 meadows of Heaven,

Blossomed the lovely stars,
 the forget-me-nots of the Angels.

> Henry Wadsworth Longfellow

ଞ ♦ ଓ

Little things
On Little Wings
Bear Little Souls to Heaven

> Anonymous

ଞ ♦ ଓ

Keep clean, bear fruit, earn life and watch
Till the white winged reapers come.

> Henry Vaughan (1625—1695)

ଞ ♦ ଓ

Go face the fire at sea, or the cholera in your
friend's house, or the burglar in your own, or
what danger lies in the way of duty, knowing you
are guarded by the Cherubim of Destiny.

> Ralph Waldo Emerson

Look homeward Angel, now, and melt with ruth.

John Milton

ဢ ◆ ႘

All God's Angels come to us disguised.

James Russell Lowell

ဢ ◆ ႘

None sing so wildly well
As the angel Israfel
And the giddy stars (so legends tell)
Ceasing their hymns, attend the spell
Of his voice, all mute.

Edgar Allan Poe

ဢ ◆ ႘

Good-night, sweet prince,
And flights of angels sing thee to thy rest!

William Shakespeare

First Degree Encounters:
Synchronicity

I feel obligated to offer a brief chapter on Synchronicity because it is the most fundamental way Angels communicate with us. It is also very personal, and difficult to describe. Synchronicity has to be experienced and explored on an individual level. Synchronisms affect the decisions we make in life, and point us in the direction we ought to take. They can carry us over difficult times, and help us overcome challenges and obstacles. While I will not go into detail on specific incidences of synchronicity (what is meaningful to me would have no significance for most of you), I will say that they have been plentiful in my life, and much more so since I made the decision to move to Maine. Because of them, I have no doubt that I am where I should be, and that I am doing what I should be doing.

If you've ever had the feeling that there was something more to certain coincidences than just random chance, you're in good company. Psychologist Carl Jung thought so, too. He named this "something more" *synchronicity* in a lengthy study published in 1955.

Jung defined synchronicity as involving "the peculiar interdependent relationship of two or more events whose connection is apparent to the observer, but whose relationship cannot be explained by the principles of causality."

More simply put, a synchronism is a coincidence (or series of them) for which you recognize that strange "something more". You generally don't have to search for this recognition; it comes to you much in the same way you experience *déja vù* (the clear but unexplainable feeling that you have been somewhere or experienced something before, when you are certain you haven't).

In her book, *Messengers of Light*, Terry Lynn Taylor describes Angels as "Synchronism Agents":

> *Not only do Angels arrange helpful coincidences,*
> *they can also use this power to send us messages.*
> *One way they communicate with us is through*
> *"synchronisms".*

It's true; if you have experienced synchronicity, you don't need me to convince you of how it has affected the direction of your life. Synchronistic occurrences in a person's life are usually a complicated string of events, each interconnected.

I am particularly fond of this quote I found in Sophy Burnham's *A Book of Angels* from an anonymous author:

> *Coincidence is God's way*
> *of performing a miracle*
> *anonymously.*

℘ ✦ ℜ

2nd Degree Encounters:
Invisible Rescues

The first time I became aware that I had been rescued by my Guardian Angel was what I call an "in-your-face" encounter—virtually impossible to ignore. Although this was not my first encounter, it was the first time I actually *realized* what had happened to me. Because of this adventure, I have since looked back on events in my life, and can identify Angelic intervention going back many years.

> In 1988, I was living in southern Florida. The entire area is peppered with many deserted roads, constructed during the 1950s by General Development in anticipation of a housing boom that never happened. These roads are so deserted that grass and weeds grow right up through the cracked asphalt, long since bleached out by the merciless sun. The road from U.S. 41 in Northport to State Road 776 in Englewood is just such a road; it's like something out of the Twilight Zone. I was reaching the Englewood end of it one afternoon on my way home from my office.

At the stop sign, I paused to turn right. As I did every day, I first looked to my left to make sure the lane I was about to enter was clear of approaching traffic. Then I looked right, and saw one car approaching from the north, some distance away. The road behind the oncoming vehicle was clear. With another quick glance to my left, I initiated my right turn.

What happened next took place so quickly that it takes much longer to tell than it did to experience.

To my horror, another vehicle had come "from out of nowhere" and was passing the approaching car at a very high speed. This car was already *in my lane,* inches from a collision with the driver's side of my car.

I felt a rush of adrenaline. I tried to think but there was no time to react. I knew there was nowhere to go. If I pulled to the left, I would collide with the first car; if I pulled right, I would plummet down into a steep drainage ditch; if I did nothing, that passing vehicle would hit me head-on doing over 50 miles an hour.

"Oh, God!" I cried out, closing my eyes. I tightened my grip on the steering wheel and prepared for impact, certain I was facing a hideous death less than a mile from home.

My eyes were closed only for an instant, but in that instant, an eerie feeling came over me. I felt something wrap around me, soft as a cloud, not really touching me, but close enough to make my skin break out in mild goose bumps.

This startled me, and I quickly opened my eyes.

I found myself alone on State Road 776. No other vehicles were in sight.

My knees were shaking and my heart was pounding. Had that passing car *passed right through my car?* Or had I been removed from the scene and returned when the danger had passed? Either way was impossible! All the way home, I kept muttering out loud, "I should be dead. I should be dead."

As I pulled into my garage, I became very calm; a sense of peace washed over me. I realized for the first time that my Guardian Angel had taken control of the situation when I could not. I walked into the house and announced to my husband, "I should be dead. There is no question in my mind that I should be dead this minute. Why was I saved?"

It has taken me a long time to discover the answer to that question. But I have no doubt that I was the recipient of an Invisible Rescue that night.

છ♦ભ

One of the most dramatic cases of Invisible Rescues happened to a friend of mine from Liberty. Karen Southworth is a gifted stained-glass artist. Not content with customary approaches, Karen constantly pushes the envelope of creativity with glass. Her work is mostly three-dimensional, and she avoids working from patterns. Some of her best work, she confesses, she does not remember creating.

In my home office where I write, I have a wonderful 3-D stained glass Angel, fashioned by Karen, presented to me as a gift shortly after I announced my intention to write *Angel Country*.

I had only known Karen a few months when I divulged my plan to write this book. That's when I heard about Karen's incredible experience; one she knows was orchestrated by her Guardian Angel. The likelihood is hard to ignore.

My family was still living in western Connecticut. One summer night, my friend Laurie and I were dressing and primping to go out. It was so hot that sweat was pouring off us as we applied makeup and tried to do something with soggy hair.

All the time we were getting ready, I kept having the same thought repeat in my mind, *We shouldn't be going out, we should just stay right here.* When I told Laurie of my apprehension, she insisted we would be fine. "I don't know," I protested, "I've got a funny feeling." She dismissed it as silly. So I pushed my "funny feeling" away and ignored the warning.

We went to a bar about twenty minutes from my house. We were having a good time when my brother walked in. Another warning bell sounded in my head—*Kurt never comes to this bar*, I thought. But he just walked in and right up to me and said, "Promise me you won't go to New York state tonight." He was so insistent. I *was* going to New York, but I lied to him and promised not to go.

As soon as my brother left, Laurie and I got in my car—a "big old bomb" Impala convertible, and drove to another bar over the New York state line. We were having fun and talking to people; I remember talking with a guy named Ricky just before the bar closed. It was about 2:00 a.m., and we got in my car and headed back to Connecticut on Route 6; a poorly-lit two-lane highway.

We were making conversation, and I remember making a turn. Suddenly, the lights went out. There hadn't been any street lights, but now I had no headlights, no dashboard lights, nothing. We were in pitch darkness.

I could feel myself going over to the right-hand side, then somehow overcorrecting for the turn, and I turned to Laurie and heard myself say, "Here we go."

The next thing I knew, the car was sitting high in the branches of this huge pine tree. (Later, I found out the car had crossed the road, gone back *up* the road, and somehow was propelled up in the air.) I remember sitting there, up in the air in this tree, feeling my face. I could feel blood all over, and I kept thinking, *I've got to get out of this car.*

I struggled to free my elbow; it was wedged in the door. The collision had pushed the engine right into the passenger compartment and it was sitting on my knees. I couldn't open the door. I couldn't even move. But I felt no pain—no pain at all.

I had the strangest feeling. It felt like I was being lifted up by unseen hands, lifting me up out of the car and then gently letting me down to the ground. It was just as if someone was carrying me as I seemed to float around to the back of the car.

There were no street lights anywhere, but it was as bright as it could be. I remember looking back over my right shoulder at a brilliant light. From within this light, I somehow found the strength to lift these huge tree limbs off the car to drag Laurie out; and I remember opening the car door and something— somebody?—helping me get her out and down to the ground.

As I sat Laurie down at the side of the road, I noticed a car stopped in the street. I went over to the car and peered inside. I can remember putting my hand on the windshield and thinking, *Uh-oh, I'm getting blood all over this car.* I looked in thinking it was Ricky from the bar, but I couldn't see his face, so I said, "Ricky?"

And the man just said, "No." Then he said, "You should go and lie down now. The ambulance is on its way."

Going to lie down seemed like an excellent idea. So I very calmly lay down on the ground. I don't know how I walked, because my knees were the size of basketballs. I still had that floating feeling. It was as though I was being brought through all these movements. At the time, everything seemed very normal to me: getting out of the car, going over and pulling these limbs off the car, dragging Laurie out of the car—like I did this every day and I didn't have to think about whether I *could* do any of it. It was so dark everywhere, but I couldn't get over the light around the car.

Lying down, I began to think: *Well, okay, who called the ambulance? Where did that car come from? Who was the driver? Why didn't he wait for the ambulance to arrive? He just said "Go lie down; the ambulance is on its way."*

I didn't have a clue who he had been.

Then the ambulance arrived, and I could hear Laurie screaming because she was bleeding. I knew my face was split wide open. My shoes were off. I was spitting out hunks of teeth and giggling because it reminded me of some Laurel and Hardy comedy routine. And I was *so calm*. I knew–*I just knew*–that I wasn't there alone.

I heard one of the paramedics say, "I don't know about this one over here. I don't think she's gonna make it."

I sat up and yelled, "The hell I'm not!"

In the hospital, my feeling of being protected continued. Although my face required two hundred stitches, I was unaware of pain, fear or anxiety. I can only describe the feeling as being embraced. I know I was surrounded by an Angelic presence. It stayed with me until my father arrived at the hospital. As soon as we made eye contact, I started to cry and get real upset. Seeing my dad shocked me back into this world. The Angels were gone; with them went the sense of comfort and peace. Even though my dad was there, it wasn't the same as having those wings wrapped around me.

That was a long time ago. But I still think about that bright light often, and I marvel. And whenever I think about it, I just say, "Thank you. Thank you."

ℰℴ✦ℭℛ

A peculiar aspect of Invisible Rescues (in fact, common to many Angelic interventions) is that there are frequently eyewitnesses to the event. Practically every contributor to this book has offered witnesses able to substantiate the experience. This helps lend credibility to the recipients when they go through the inevitable *"I must have imagined it"* stage.

From Kathy Davis (not her real name) of Thomaston, comes a remarkable tale of Angelic rescue that not only saved the lives of four children, but had a profound effect on the spiritual lives of the adults they would become.

When I was a child, my grandparents had a cottage on Fish Pond in South Hope. When I was about ten years old, we spent Mother's Day there. It was still too cold to put the boats in the water, but my two brothers, my sister and I had this homemade raft, and we took it out on the water. The name "pond" is misleading, because Fish Pond is quite a large body of water—over a mile long and nearly half a mile wide. To four children between the ages of five and ten, it was absolutely huge.

We were using a stick to propel the raft across the pond; we were playing and having a good time. Until the stick got stuck in the mud. The raft with all of us kids got free and we began floating toward the middle of the pond.

The wind was blowing pretty hard, and as we approached the middle of the pond, we realized that the raft was sinking. Water was up to our ankles and we were terrified. None of us could swim. We started to scream for help. My grandparents heard us hollering and they came down toward the pond. They could see us and they were desperate—they had to run about a quarter of a mile up the dirt road to the nearest neighbor's house to borrow a canoe. We didn't know it then, but grandmother was praying as they carried the canoe down to the pond to rescue us.

We all knew that the raft was sinking. We were all so afraid. But I was the oldest, and I tried to hide my fear. I told my brothers and sister, "We need to pray."

So we prayed, the way only kids can, out of desperation and from the heart. We reached out to God. We promised Him that we would read the entire Bible from cover to cover if He would save us.

Suddenly, the sinking raft began to head back toward the shore. The wind had shifted for no apparent reason. It didn't blow us all the way to land, but close enough to shore that we could get off safely. The adventure wasn't over quite so easily—it took us three hours to trek through the woods back to the cottage, but none of us really got hurt.

To this day, we all look at that event as being miraculous.

Both my brothers and my sister are still alive and can verify that this happened to us. My sister attends church faithfully and is raising her children within the church. My brother is a born-again believer, deeply involved with his church, and my own children and I have also been quite involved with our church.

I think I am the only one of the four who has yet to fulfill that promise we all made; I have not forgotten it, and it does tug at my conscience periodically. I do plan to keep my promise, because God kept his that day.

Those children didn't know anything about physical laws. They were unaware that while the wind can push a floating object easily, it's a very different story when that object is sinking under the weight of four bodies. But they recognized a miracle when they saw one!

෨♦ෛ

3rd Degree Encounters:
Auditory

S ome of the most frequent Angelic episodes I have come across are those that involve "the Voice".

It will be easy to discern from the following stories that I am not talking about people who are led through their lives by constant voices instructing them in abhorrent behavior—that is a symptom of schizophrenia, a psychological disorder which is not in any way connected to anything Angelic.

The Voice may come in words, or other sounds, and has a mission to accomplish. That mission is frequently to get your attention and alert you to something that could cause you harm. Whether it's a voice you hear "in your head", or one that seems to come from without, the Voice makes its presence known briefly, forcefully, and, having accomplished its task, quickly departs.

My husband, Frank, had a recent encounter with such a Voice that became the impetus for this book. Although both of us have experienced Angelic intervention on numerous occasions, this one finally got my attention, and became the inspiration for this project.

When Frank expressed to me that he had been feeling a little anxious about his new job, I offered him some advice to comfort him. I told him whenever he felt stressed to picture himself surrounded with Angelic protection. I prayed to my Angel to send for "reinforcements" to encircle him with peace.

The next night, he had an extraordinary story to tell me.

At 6:30 in the morning, there is not much traffic on U.S. 1 headed toward Camden. Driving to work, I had been thinking about what my wife had said about imagining myself surrounded with Angels.

As I approached Powerhouse Hill from the south, I suddenly heard a Voice in my car.

Now, this was no ordinary voice. It was so powerful, my whole body began to vibrate from the sound. It was like a thousand voices shouting all at once; it certainly got my attention! I was sure it was all the same voice, the same timbre; I think if you could map it, it would show up as one voice print. When you hear a voice like that, you listen.

The Voice said—with authority and urgency— *"Pull over to the right!"*

This Voice wanted me to pull over, and it wanted me to pull over NOW! It didn't care that I was doing 45 miles an hour, approaching a hill. I knew I'd heard that Voice before, and I had learned to trust it. So without hesitation, I quickly pulled onto the soft shoulder, and slowed down to about 5 mph.

As my car crawled along on the shoulder, I was thinking: *I wonder what that was all about?*

As I looked up, I was startled to see a car coming from just over the crest of the hill in front of me. It was speeding toward me, barreling down the hill out of control, headed right for me in the wrong lane—the same lane that the Voice had urged me out of moments before!

I stepped on my brake, and the oncoming car whizzed by mine. I could feel a great whoosh of air as it passed me—it came so close to me that it nearly took off my side view mirror. I was glad I don't drive with my arm out the window—I surely would've lost it in that moment.

It was then I noticed a police car had been waiting at the stop sign at Old County Road, just below the crest of the hill. The cruiser turned south in pursuit of the speeder, siren blaring and lights flashing. In my rear view mirror, I could see that the police car had stopped the driver before he could kill someone. The driver hadn't even pulled over when he heard the siren—he just stopped in the middle of the road.

I know that if I had not listened to the Voice, I would have been in the path of that speeding vehicle, and would not have survived to tell the tale. I took a deep breath and said a silent prayer of thanks to my Guardian Angel before continuing on to work.

And I stopped worrying needlessly about my job.

80✦03

Dorothy Jordan of Warren is a firm believer in Angels. She shared two vivid experiences with me. One is a classic Fifth Degree Encounter, described later in *Angel Country*. This one involves the Voice.

> One day while I was driving my car about 55 mph, I heard a distinct voice in my car say, *"Slow Down!"*
>
> I obeyed, and slowed to 35 mph.
>
> The Voice came again. *"Slow Down!"*
>
> I slowed again, this time to 15 mph.
>
> A car was coming toward me in the other lane and the road went around a sharp corner. As I came around the curve, I suddenly saw two small children playing in the street directly ahead of me. Because I was only going 15 mph, I was able to react quickly and stop my car to avoid hitting them.
>
> I know that if that Voice hadn't slowed me down, I would not have been able to avoid killing them both!

ℰℴ✦ℭℛ

While researching this book, I have become acquainted with many new and wonderful people. One of the most remarkable is Woodrow Wilson Richards of Milo. Woody's life has been chock-full of spiritual encounters, and you will find two of them in *Angel Country*. Woody has been bountifully blessed, and I have reaped the rewards of those blessings by my association with this gentle, soft-spoken man. His experiences cover the spectrum of all degrees of Angelic encounters, and a few that defy categorization.

Woody Richards came into my life shortly after WABI (Channel 5 in Bangor) broadcast my story, in early April of 1995. His help in producing this book has been immeasurable. You will learn more about Woody later in *Angel Country*, but right here I want to share Woody's death at the age of nineteen with you.

> When I was nineteen, I fell off a truck into a flume; it is like a man-made river about twenty feet wide and ten feet deep—full of logs which I had been unloading when I fell into the water. When I tried to climb up onto a log, another one would fall on top of me and knock me off. After a few attempts, I would hold myself stiff and sink to the bottom, then jump up and try to swim through the thick log jam. Once I got through, but another log just knocked me under again. After five or six tries, I was getting tired, and realized to keep trying was hopeless. But I was determined to keep trying until I die.

> While I was under the water, out of breath, trying to think what to do (because I knew death was imminent)—should I take a deep breath of water, or try to hold out? There was no choice, really, because I couldn't hold out.

> Suddenly, a Voice, very powerful (but not at all frightening) said, *"If you want to live, hold your breath and pass out."*

> I didn't think this would work, but with no choices left, I decided to give it my best.

> Sometime later (minutes, I think), my eyes opened up, and I saw a pulp hook with a rope tied to it hanging in front of me. I wasn't breathing and I couldn't move, just see.

> The Voice came back.

"Take the hook and put it through your clothing, a place strong enough to support your weight. Do not hang on, because you're going to pass out again."

I thought, *I can't move.*

The Voice said: *"Take your left hand, reach out and take the hook."*

I reached out with my left hand ("he" helped me) and jabbed the hook into my right collar area. I seemed to know that was a strong cloth area. My head could only stare straight ahead as I poked around. I wondered about jabbing myself, because the hook was sharp.

The Voice:

"Even if you do, it's a minor wound."

(Later I found out that the hook had barely scratched my shoulder.)

The next thing I remember, I was lying on the ground. With my eyes closed, I saw two men looking down at me, and a third man was running toward us. When he got to where we were, he asked the other two men (one of them was my boss) what happened. They told him I was dead; that I had fallen into the flume and was underwater for over six minutes. They had pulled me out with a rope and a hook. They were sure I was dead anyway so it wouldn't matter where the hook got me. I watched as they walked away from me. I felt no pain or anything, just frustration because I couldn't move, not even a finger.

The next thing I remember, I was in an ambulance. They're quite noisy, and I woke up from the noise. I was lying on a narrow cot. There was a man sitting on my left and another up by my head—I could see them both without moving. They were both looking out the back door windows. I didn't know why I was there; I was in no pain. I wondered why they were looking out the back window. I wanted to see, too. So I sat up to look.

"Jesus!" one hollered, and both of them jumped. The one behind me laid me down. I guess they figured out I wasn't dead, after all.

My next memory was being back in the water, fighting to get out of that cloudy water again, and struggling to move the logs that were on top of me. It turned out I was actually fighting off nurses who were trying to hold me down. I realized then that I was in a hospital, covered with an oxygen tent.

A day or two later, I checked myself out of the hospital. I still don't know why. It was my first hospital visit; I guess I didn't like it there. I recall a man in an office explaining that if I left, I was on my own, not his responsibility. I think I signed something. I wasn't worried; I knew something that they didn't know. I was being watched over.

Still am.

§∂♦Q

Thirty years later, the Voice saved Woody's life again.

About fifteen years ago, I was driving truck from Maine to Canada, hauling chips. About halfway, in the County, I passed a house whose mailbox had the same last name as mine. You know that little curious feeling you have when this happens?

I thought that maybe some evening when I wasn't in a hurry, I might stop and talk to these people.

Well, about a month later one Friday around 5:00 p.m., I had some time to spare; didn't have enough time for another load, so I thought I might stop and introduce myself to whoever lived there.

As I approached this place, I could see a car in the yard, and I thought that at this time of day on a Friday the man of the house might be home. As I slowed down to stop, I felt a strong sense that I should keep on going. I didn't pay much attention to this feeling, thinking the sense meant beware of a dog or something. So I pulled over, close to their mailbox. As I opened the door to get out, I was looking toward the house to see if anyone was going to come out to greet me.

Just then, a Voice in my head said, *"Get out of here! Get this truck going now!"*

I suddenly felt afraid and a little bewildered, but I'd heard this Voice before, so I quickly shut the door and drove away, thinking there must have been a pack of ugly dogs there.

As soon as I got out of sight of the house, a great feeling of relief came over me. Not really knowing what it was all about, I more or less put the idea of stopping there out of my mind, even though I drove past two or three times a week.

About three years later, I was working in a factory. I had been there about six months, and got so I knew the whole crew (on my floor, anyway) on a first-name basis. Five or so of us guys were sitting around at dinnertime discussing women, wives, etc. One guy was telling a story about how his wife had run off with some truck driver and how he almost shot some dumb trucker just for stopping in front of his house.

A bell went off in my head. I asked him his last name; it was the same as mine. I asked if he lived in a certain place, and described where I had stopped that time three years earlier, down to the side of the road and description of the house, etc. His eyes opened wide, and he asked, "How do you know that?" I kept on asking questions: "Was that a red Dodge 18-wheeler?"

He stopped eating. "How would you know all that?" he demanded.

I told him that the person in that red truck was me, and that I had stopped only because his last name was the same as mine, and I thought we might have had an interesting conversation. I knew nothing about his wife, but I had a funny feeling to leave, so I did.

He lowered his eyes and said, "Boy, it's a good thing you left because I had a rifle trained on your head. I just hated any trucker that went by, and when one stopped, I thought, *This one's asking for it.* I was drunk and stupid. A couple of days later, I sobered up and realized what I almost did."

I laughed and said, "Well, I'm glad I had a feeling to leave." I didn't explain about the Voice in my head; I just left it at that. But I did ask him, "If I had gotten out of the truck, would you have pulled the trigger?"

He gave me a sorrowful look, and replied, "Yes." He was hurt, drunk, and full of hate, and he was thinking, *As soon as that trucker's feet hit the ground, I'll blow him away.*

I said, "But you would have shot an innocent person." He replied, "I knew that. At least a couple of days later I did, and I was thankful that trucker drove away."

"Me, too!" I said, and everyone laughed.

Later, I got to know this man, and I felt he was a nice fella, and honest; about my age. And I understood the feelings he had at that time, and I do believe he would have pulled the trigger. I thank God and my Guardian Angel for getting me out of there. I was safe, and a nice person didn't have to go to prison.

My Angel—my friend—saved two of us at the same time. And I'm thankful.

ℰ◆ℛ

A few years ago, Woody Richards discovered a new talent. He began to manifest a gift for healing others, guided by his Angelic friends. I have personally witnessed some of these amazing healings and have documented many testimonials from others who have been helped by Woody's gift. He gives all credit to his "Friends", as he calls his Angels. He attempts to help all who come to him for healing, and asks no monetary reward for his efforts (although donations are appreciated). Space does not allow me to go into too many details about this subject in *Angel Country*. I expect I will probably have to devote an entire book to chronicling Woody's Adventures in Angel Land someday soon. (Fortunately for me, he has kept detailed journals of his experiences over the years!)

ℰ◆ℛ

In the foregoing examples, I've shown you how listening to "the Voice" has saved lives. Now I want to show you how it radically *changed* a life.

Sixty years ago, Munjoy Hill was Portland's Italian neighborhood. John Ricci admits that when he was growing up there, he and his friends were definitely no angels.

> When I was in the third grade, my friends and I used to hang out at McCarthy's grocery store all the time, raising hell. One day, for reasons known only to him, Eddie McCarthy started calling me "Wahoo".

> Pretty soon, all the kids were calling me Wahoo, too. One day I asked Eddie who Wahoo was. He answered, "He's your Guardian Angel." Maybe he was making it up, fooling around, making a joke—I don't know. But I was eight years old, and still young enough not to question anything a grownup told me. It never occurred to me that what he said was other than the truth.

> Not long after, in Catechism class, the nun was teaching a lesson on Guardian Angels. She asked the class, "Who has a Guardian Angel?" I knew this one! My hand shot right up. "I do!" I yelled, "He's an Indian named Wahoo!"

> All the kids laughed, but the nun did not. I got whacked. I was surprised, because I was sure I had the right answer. (I guess the answer was supposed to be, "We *all* have a Guardian Angel.") Anyway, when I got home, my father gave me a whipping, too. Needless to say, I was pretty confused.

> Well, I grew up and forgot all about Wahoo. But he hadn't forgotten me.

I guess you could say I led a sort of charmed life. I know I've been lucky all my life. By the time I was a man, I was pretty much a wiseguy; my good luck followed me and I guess it made me cocky. I had earned a rather, shall we say, unsavory reputation. And I certainly wasn't much of what you would call religious.

One day I was taking my aunt to visit the cemetery. Suddenly, I heard a voice in my head, very clear. It said, *"Don't go back."* I knew exactly what this meant; I was facing a crossroads in my life and had been trying to make a decision. The voice was definitely Indian. I knew then it must be Wahoo. I followed his advice, and because I did, my good luck got even better. I eventually met and married the wonderful woman who is now my wife, and I have a terrific daughter. I have survived a massive heart attack and open heart surgery. And I have enjoyed financial security.

But Wahoo wasn't through with me yet. Like I said, I had a bad reputation. Make of that what you will. About twenty years ago, I returned from Massachusetts determined to make a killing in real estate. I decided to buy an old nursing home and turn it into an apartment house. The owner of the building was a gambler and wanted to unload the property. No problem?

Problem.

There were seventeen residents in this nursing home. I couldn't wait to get these people out and renovate the building. The State was funding these patients' care, but it sure didn't look like they were receiving any of it. These poor people were living in absolutely deplorable conditions; too awful to describe. *Too bad*, I thought, *they're not my problem*. I just wanted those people out of my building.

One night, I was awakened out of a sound sleep. It was Wahoo. *"Don't turn your back on those people,"* he said. *"You can't throw them out. You have to take care of them."*

Take care of them! I wanted to get rid of them! Well, I thought; maybe I could let them stay until the State finds another place to put them. These were *my* thoughts; it was not what Wahoo had in mind. "Another place to put them" never materialized.

I didn't know the first thing about running a nursing home. But I learned fast. Once again, Wahoo had turned my life around.

I found I really enjoyed caring for those people. It made me feel good. I didn't take a penny out of the business for seven years, and I continued to run it for seventeen years. By the time I retired, I owned two successful nursing homes.

My friends used to joke about the "new" me. They called me "Boy Scout". I enjoyed it so much that I found an old picture of myself in a Boy Scout uniform taken when I was fourteen years old. I had it blown up and hung it behind my desk in my office at the nursing home.

One day I was having a conversation in my office with Paul Davis, a soap salesman. The subject somehow got around to Guardian Angels. I told Paul about my Guardian Angel being an Indian named Wahoo. Paul leaned forward and said, "I see you've got a picture of him, too!"

I didn't know what he was talking about. But I turned around to look at the Boy Scout picture. Sure enough, there beside my left foot, was an Indian, wearing a buffalo robe. As I stared at the photograph in amazement, I heard Wahoo say, *"Didn't you know I was here?"*

I'm retired now, and I still feel lucky. I'm definitely not crazy or weird. And yes, I still have that picture.

🕛♦℞

4th Degree Encounters:
Apparitions & Dreams

T he very first story I received came from Everett (Melvin) Cross of Brewer. It is a powerful story of miraculous healing, and involves an apparition which I interpret as a manifestation of the Archangel Raphael. The name Raphael means "God Heals" or "Divine Healer". Raphael directs his healing beams into hospitals, homes and hearts where they are needed. His symbol is a magnificent sword; and he is associated with all shades of the color blue.

Everett knows he received a miracle, and because of it, he has been able to realize that many other miracles have happened in his life. He has shared these with me so that I may share them with you.

> In August of 1994, I was released from the hospital after surgery on an artery in my neck. That same night, I got out of my bed shortly after midnight and walked over to my wife's bed. She saw that something was wrong with me. My eyes were staring straight ahead and I was talking gibberish, saying the same thing over and over again. My wife called 911.

I woke up in the hospital some eight hours later, almost as if I had never left. I had suffered a stroke. I could see my heartbeat on the heart monitor was almost a flat line, but wavering slightly, like a slow wave. I couldn't talk without garbling my words; I couldn't move, I couldn't even think very well. My whole family was there—they thought I was a goner. My daughters had come from Texas, and my son who is a minister was there, too. I confessed my sins and waited to die.

Some time later, I woke up and looked at the monitor. I saw that the soft wavy line was gone, and in its place, the line had become like peaks, and then more lines appeared—it looked like a normal heartbeat should. The room was filled with light. Suddenly, I looked up and clearly saw a two-edged sword, glowing blue around the edges, hovering above my bed and pointing at me. I tried to tell my wife, but she couldn't see it.

I began to recover rapidly. Before, I couldn't walk or talk, I couldn't write, or even add. Now I am doing all these things.

When I came home from the hospital, I found a book (*The Power of Prayer* by E.M. Bounds) with a page my father had marked for me. When I read it, my heart leaped. The passage goes,

> *A two-edged sword of heavenly tempered steel...comes in answer to prayer; it impregnates, succors, softens, soothes. It carries the Word like dynamite...it is a gift from God.*

That two-edged sword *was* a gift from God, and I know a miracle happened to me. I began writing poetry, and I have even had some published.

I tell this story to anyone who will listen to me. God gave me a gift. He gave me back my life, and I am going to give that gift back to everyone who needs it.

Since his amazing recovery, Everett has become an accomplished poet. I am delighted to publish one of his most powerful and touching poems.

The Debt That I Owe

by Everett M. Cross

If I have strength, I owe service of the strong.
If a melody I have, then I owe them a song.
If I can stand, when others around me are falling
If I can hurry when needy souls are calling
And if my touch can warm those in the cold,
Then I must pay the debt that I owe.
If Heaven's grace has given to me some gift
If I can move some load no other can lift
If I can help some wound no other can heal,
If some message of Hope I can reveal
Then with Courage and Faith, through Life I must go
And pay to Mankind the debt that I owe.
For any talent God gives to me, I cannot pay
Gifts are mine only when I give them away.
Heaven's gifts are like flowers that bloom in the sun
They gladly give their beauty to everyone.
The riches of love are far better than gold.
So I must go pay the debt that I owe.

෫෮ ♦ ෬෫

In June, 1994, a collision at the intersection of Routes 11 and 43 in Exeter demolished two pickup trucks and sent four people to Eastern Maine Medical Center. A truck driven by a Harrington man failed to stop at a stop sign, and collided with the truck belonging to Gerald and Bonnie Coombs of Garland.

The photo in the *Bangor Daily News* shows the Coombs' truck resting on its roof between two large trees, where it landed after it shot into a ditch and rolled over. From the position of the truck, it is apparent that it could not have "rolled" between the trees; it had to have tumbled in *end over end*. According to the Maine State Trooper at the scene, none of the four had been wearing a seat belt. When I saw this photograph, I was astonished that anyone even survived the crash. (All four did.)

Bonnie Coombs is no stranger to adversity. Widowed in 1988, when her husband of seventeen years fell out of a boat during an epileptic seizure, she raised her two sons (one also epileptic) alone for six years. In April of 1994, she married Jerry Coombs, whom she had known since she was sixteen. They were newlyweds out for a Sunday drive when their lives turned, literally, upside down.

> We had gotten up at about 6:00 a.m. and decided to go for a ride to Belfast; I don't remember much that went on. I do remember that I was half sleeping, and I never felt the collision at all. The only thing I knew was that the truck was rolling over.
>
> In my mind, I was thinking—*Jerry, what did you do?*— but he later told me I yelled it out at him. When the truck stopped, I just got out of the window as fast as I could. I looked in, Jerry was all blood; I thought he was gone. I was so scared, I felt like my whole body was racing. Then I heard him say, "I'm stuck!"

I felt like a hand just picked me up and carried me over to the driver's side.

I could see the gas was running out of the truck pretty fast. A witness told my son Daniel that he yelled at me, "Lady, get away from the truck!" He said I turned around and looked right at him with glassy eyes and just said, "NO!"

I went back to the other side, and was trying to help Jerry out. I could hear the woman from the other truck yelling, but it seemed a million miles away. I know I screamed, "Somebody, please help him!" Jerry said it was a good thing I did, because it made him realize that no one was coming to help, so he began pushing and managed to free himself.

After I saw that he was out and talking, I just felt so *tired*. I don't actually remember sitting or lying down, but I do remember being *on* the ground. I don't remember what I *said*, but I sure remember what I *saw*.

Jerry said I had my hands up in the air and said, "Ooh...Jerry, look at the pretty Angel!"

I saw a very bright light, and a woman in a long white robe with some sort of corded belt around her; her feet were bare. I don't know if her hair was white or blonde, but it was very long. She held her arms out toward me, and smiled. She never spoke, but her eyes seemed to tell me, *"You don't have to be afraid. Everything's going to be all right. We're here to help you."*

I felt so at peace. She stayed only a short time, but then I saw Bob (my first husband). Now I know people think I'm crazy, that I was hallucinating. But I know what I saw and heard. He was standing near a very bright light. He had on a work shirt, jeans and work boots. He smiled, and told me, *"I am fine and happy. It's not your time yet. You must go back; you have our sons to take of. They both need you. Remember that I'll always be watching over you."*

From what seemed like very far away, I could hear people yelling, "Bonnie! Bonnie!" and I became aware that someone was slapping my face gently. I opened my eyes. I saw Jerry and other people standing over me. I heard someone say, "She says she saw an Angel. Or thinks she did." I know the peaceful, at-rest feeling was gone; I could feel the pain. I was hurting so bad. I did not want to come back; I thought, *If it feels that peaceful to die, then I'm not scared to go.*

At the hospital, I was scared for Jerry. They took him ahead of me and I'd only seen him for a minute before they took him to the operating room. I know he was worrying about me, too. I told a nurse, "I saw an Angel." She looked at me like I'd "lost it," and just said, "You'll be okay." I told other people I had seen an Angel. Everyone looked at me that same way. I know no one believed me; some even made fun and had little smart things to say. But it's okay.

Jerry believed me. He said, "It must be true; I saw you put your hands up."

After this accident, I remembered that four years earlier, I had fallen asleep while driving from Augusta to Dexter and totaled my truck. I saw an Angel in a bright flash then, too. I think God is trying hard to tell me something; maybe to change my life, I don't know. But seeing that Angel sure made my life different; I do know that I look at things a lot different than before.

ဆာ◆က

N ot all Third Degree encounters are as spectacular as Everett's or Bonnie's. Some can be momentary, and don't seem (at the time) to have much consequence. Nevertheless, they linger in our conscious memories, and we still remember them many years later.

Many adults recall early childhood experiences with Angels. And it is often far into adulthood that they realize that the experience wasn't "real" or "normal". Children are exceptionally perceptive to spiritual encounters; they are innocent of deception and have not yet been conditioned by adults to disbelieve. To children, everything is *real*; they are unable to distinguish between "reality" and "apparition". Jesus said, "Suffer little children to come unto me...for such is the Kingdom of God," (Mark, 10:14). He was acknowledging how special and receptive the souls of children are to miracles, large or small.

ဆာ◆က

G ail Schatzle of Bethel wrote, "I don't know if this counts, but I can remember the "White Lady" visiting me in my bedroom when I was about four years old." Gail says she doesn't remember much else, but she does not associate the memory with fear, only warm comforting feelings. I say, if you remember something so miniscule for forty years, IT COUNTS.

ဆာ◆က

Marilyn Wiggin of Portland wrote to tell me of her experience when she was a small child. Although this happened many years ago, it is still very clear to her now.

It was Christmas time. When most children are anticipating the Christmas holiday, I was too ill to take an interest in anything at that time.

I had pneumonia with a very high fever and was not expected to live. Until one night, I awoke in the middle of the night and glanced over to the door. As I did, there appeared to be a lady, almost transparent, hovering in mid-air, in the doorway. She wore a long flowing dress and had long hair. I remember how beautiful and peaceful looking she was and everything about her was in a white glow. She was holding what appeared to be a needle in her hand and I suddenly felt the impact of something going through my arm. The next thing I remember was waking up the next morning, and to the surprise of my parents, my fever had broken and I was well again soon after.

When I told others about what had happened that particular night, they did not take it seriously. But to this day, I have no doubt in my mind that it was my Guardian Angel who saved my life—good medicine!

ℬ♦ℭ

About a month after I began asking the people of Maine to share their Angelic Encounters with me, I was surprised to receive a letter from Pennsylvania. The story it tells took place in Rockland, and it touched me deeply. This Angelic apparition purchased five years for a young girl to build a relationship with a father she had barely known. This letter came from Sherry Stine.

> My father, Ira Tupper, was born and raised on Vinalhaven, and lived all his adult life in Rockland. His name was known to many, because he was an alcoholic and the town drunk. He struggled all his life with this disease, but was unable to fight his demons. He eventually died from alcohol-related causes.
>
> He had a drinking problem long before I was born. Over the years, his drinking was taking his mind and body, and we knew if he didn't quit soon it would be too late. Although he had been in and out of detox programs repeatedly, he couldn't quit.
>
> Quite suddenly, in 1976, he stopped drinking.
>
> It was very hard on him at first. He was nervous and shaky, but he appeared to be making it. I felt so lucky, because I was building a relationship with my father for the first time. We had many conversations, and I learned how my father thought and felt about things that happened to him in his life.
>
> During one of our great conversations, I asked him what it was that helped him quit drinking. He told me that on this one particular day, he had gone to the liquor store and bought a pint to take to the Public Landing to drink. He said it was a bright, sunny day, and he was lying on the grass when he looked up across the bay. He said he saw three Angels coming across the water. When he saw that, he knew that if he didn't quit drinking, he was going to die.

Now I know some would say that he was in a drunken state and didn't know what he was doing. But I really believed my father when he said he saw these Angels. He stated it so matter-of-factly. After all these years, I still believe he saw something that moved him spiritually. My father didn't take another drink for five years.

Unfortunately, he did begin drinking again and became sicker and sicker. But those five years were the only time in his life that he quit, and for those five years of my life, I had a father.

℠◆℣

Martha S. of Rockport knows she is protected by a Guardian Angel. She wrote to tell me of two memorable experiences she had which helped her to understand his presence and loving care.

In February of 1986, I was six months pregnant with my first child. I had been told that I had to have surgery for a hernia which might complicate my pregnancy and jeopardize my delivery. I was extremely apprehensive and nervous. I was concerned that the baby would be harmed or that I might miscarry.

A few days before the scheduled surgery, I was taking a rest in our apartment. My husband was in the living room; I was lying on our bed, in our bedroom. I was sideways, my back facing the open bedroom door. I thought I heard or felt someone entering the room. Thinking it was my husband checking on me, I didn't do anything, but as the seconds passed and I still felt the presence of someone staring at me, I turned my head toward the door. It wasn't my husband, but the image or person of a woman. The only part I could not see, because it was blacked out, was the face. I say it was a woman because it seemed to be my height, with long, shoulder-length hair of dark brown or black. She was wearing a white flowing dress with long sleeves. It was very white. The person was very close to my bed, so I turned toward her some more to see better. She didn't speak, but I had the most peaceful feeling overcome me. It was so tranquil. I felt very safe, and I knew then that everything was going to be all right during my surgery, and that I need not worry about anything. I felt so secure that I turned around and fell asleep.

I don't know how long I slept, but when I awoke, I knew I was okay and that I had not dreamt the episode. I told my husband about it. At first, I wasn't sure whether my visitor had been male or female. But after telling my husband about it, I seemed to feel that it had been my cousin who had died unexpectedly in December. She had been so excited about the birth of my baby. I believe she came to tell me that all would be well.

And it was.

℘ ♦ ℭ

I had another experience recently. In the years that have passed since my first visitation, I continue to believe and have always felt the presence of someone looking after me or keeping me company. But I had never seen anything again.

A few months ago, I woke up in the middle of the night, because I felt someone putting a blanket over me—covering me as I would my child while she slept. This was a particularly cold night. We had been having some financial worries, and I tend not to sleep very well when this occurs.

I looked up, expecting to see my husband covering me with the blanket. Instead, I saw a very tall person, a man, I thought, standing at the foot of my bed, looking at me with the most loving expression. I actually could feel the intensity of his concern and love for me. It seemed as if he was enveloping me with all those feelings and saying to me that he would take care of me, that all would get better, not to worry, to relax and everything would be okay. He communicated all this without speaking; he just stood there for what seemed to me to be a long time, gazing at me in a very loving way. Eventually, I fell asleep, and as far as I could remember, he was still there.

The next day, I asked my husband if he had put the blanket on me. When he said he hadn't, I told him what I had seen and felt. But the most wonderful thing was that I awoke with no worries whatsoever. I knew that everything was going to be all right, regardless of the financial situation we were in at the moment. I knew that things would get better and that I need not worry. I had complete trust in that person.

At first I thought it was my father, who knew of my concerns and wanted to ease my worries. Then the more I thought about it, I thought maybe it had been St. Jude, because I had been praying to him. But I recently realized that the person was my Guardian Angel. I believe this because since that night, I have on many occasions felt someone in my house when I am alone. It doesn't frighten me, because when I hear or feel that presence, it lets me know that it is my Angel and I can feel the presence of a male.

Since this last experience, I do not worry about finances as I used to. I truly believe that I should not worry, that I am being looked after and that I should not waste my energy worrying about things that someone else is looking after for me.

I tell my friends or anyone who listens that there are Angels who guide us, look after us and are here to help us if we want their help. I have taught my daughter since she was very little that she has an Angel and there is no need to be afraid at night because he is with her.

&) ✦ CR

S ome people think that we become Angels when we die. Most religious and philosophical texts, however, do not support this theory. There is considerable documentation throughout written history, and from various cultures and religions, to support the conviction that Angelic civilization existed long before Man. The Bible tells us that Man was created a little lower than the Angels (Hebrews 2:7) and put in their charge. Although we don't become Angels after death, we do join them, and get to live on the same spiritual plane with them. Angels come to escort us from this life to the next—they accompany our souls home to the dwelling place of the Creator.

In recent years, there has been much written about NDEs, or near-death experiences. Many people who have undergone the trauma of near- or clinical-death report very similar experiences of seeing the great "white light", feeling an overwhelming sense of peace and love, and being greeted by loved ones who have passed over. So many people have reported these experiences that the subject is no longer controversial. Recently, however, a faction of the scientific community began focusing on the theory that such experiences can be explained away as haphazard neural firings of a dying brain.

I believe that when a person is close to death, his Guardian Angel comes to escort the spirit across the threshold from the physical world to the spirit world. Many people fear death because it represents the unknown. To ease the trauma of the transition, your Angelic Escort comes to you wearing familiar faces.

When Maria Snow of Spruce Head wrote me, she was not certain that her experience would fall into the realm of Angelic Intervention, but it was a very powerful event in her life. Her story not only affirmed my own belief, but would seem to totally dispel that "dying brain" theory! It is truly one of the most remarkable examples of Angelic apparition I have come across.

> I am a registered nurse, having cared for the ill and dying and post-mortem detail as well.

> My mother was an intelligent and perceptive woman who had practiced clinical psychology in Connecticut for many years, prior to her early retirement in 1973.

> In January of 1993, my mother (age 71) was diagnosed with myelodisplastic illness, became transfusion dependent, and a rapid decline followed. She spent winters in Florida and summers in Maine, which she considered "home". My siblings and I had been back and forth to Florida for her increasingly frequent hospitalizations.

> Over a period of six months to a year, beginning in late 1991, my mother and I had experienced a

"falling out" of sorts. Thankfully, she and I re-sumed a close (actually, closer) relationship during her illness. My mother requested to come "home" on May 15, 1993, via airplane, wheelchair, etc. Much to our surprise, she expired on May 18. We had thought she had at least a few more months.

I transported her to Penobscot Bay Medical Center the morning of the 18th; she was oriented but very weak, with suspected internal bleeding. During her brief stay in the Special Care Unit, all of my sib-lings were with her. After some Demerol and se-vere hypoxia, she became unresponsive. The last words she said were, "I love you, Maria."

In her last few moments, I held her hand and said, "Oh, Mom, Nona (her mother) and Uncle Petey (her favorite brother, who had died in 1973) would be so proud of you."

I don't know why I said this—it didn't—and doesn't—sound like me.

Although I can't say why, I somehow knew in ad-vance that the next breath she took would be her final one. As she exhaled for the last time, it seemed more like a rather (relieved? contented?) sigh, I saw—felt? experienced? I don't know, the verb eludes me—Nona, my grandmother. The im-pression of her was very distinct. She wore a blue dress with white designs and belt, and her right arm was outstretched. Beside her, to the left and slightly behind, was Uncle Pete. He was wearing green Dickies® work pants, and jingling change in his left pocket. On his face was a look of childlike excitement or anticipation. They came out of a tunnel or hallway with a fading light behind them. The light seemed diagonal and brighter behind my grandmother. Although traumatized and devastated by the loss of my mother, I felt this experience was a gift of some sort; an assurance, a comfort—it has helped me and that is all I really know.

What a wonderful gift! Maria's mother shared with her daughter the vision of her escorting Angels! Or perhaps, it was the Angels' gift to Maria—to let her know that her mother was being welcomed home by loving spirits. Either way, it was a dynamic experience for Maria, and one she is not likely to forget.

ℰℴ✦ℭℛ

M any people have visions or dreams of loved ones who have passed over. Often the dear departed comes to offer a solution to pressing problems or to just impart a sense of "everything's okay" to those left behind. Even though I know our souls continue to exist in "heaven", I don't feel the human soul has the capacity to freely pass between the spiritual and the physical the way the Angels do. But, since human souls can dwell *among* the Angels, and on their spiritual level, there is every reason to believe they can request an Angel to deliver a heavenly message in their stead. As I stated earlier, an Angel can appear in any form it chooses; it is free to make the decision as to what form we mortals will accept as messenger.

I have always been fascinated by dreams. I have tried all the recommended methods that I have read about for remembering my dreams. Alas, try as I might, I find that I am one of those people whose dreams regularly evaporate seconds after waking. There are, however, exceptions. When I awake from a dream of my grandmother or my father, or one in which a question is answered, or some "wisdom" is imparted, I have no trouble remembering it, in detail. The memories of these dreams do not fade, and I am able to refer to them periodically to see if the meaning has some application in a given situation facing me.

I have often been visited in dreams by my grandmother, who has brought me solutions to problems (real or imagined) which were weighing heavily on my mind and heart. I know my beloved Mama watches over me, because when she wants to remind me, she sends an Angel in her form, so I will be certain the message came from her.

In 1969, when I was dating a soldier on leave from Viet Nam, Mama had said, "Nunju worry. Nikesa say the wall is over and the boysa coma home." This translates from her Sicilian-flavored English to "Don't worry. Nixon says the war is over and the boys will all come home." (My brother and I still use this phrase today, when faced with a situation that looks bleak.) My friend came back all right. Mama told the truth (even if Nixon didn't).

I was for some years a full-time musician. By the summer of 1979, I was spending more and more time "on the road", and it became impractical to keep an apartment. I moved back home with my mother, grandmother and great-aunt. One major obstacle I faced was what to do with my cat, Rogue, who had been my faithful companion for nearly ten years. My mother also had a male cat, Alex, who was very territorial. When I brought Rogue to visit, all hell broke loose between them. It was certain that I could not move home with my cat. Eventually (after considerable begging), I was able to persuade a friend to care for him.

I had moved into Mama's old room; she had recently been moved into another bedroom with her sister. She was over eighty years old and sometimes forgetful, and many nights I would hear her shuffling in the hall outside my bedroom door. She would ask, "Who'sa in my room?" When she'd open the door and see me, she would say, "Oh! It'sa you! I forget!" We'd both laugh, and I would kiss her good-night and she would go back to her new room.

Eight months after I moved home, Mama died from complications of pneumonia. I rode with her in the ambulance, and like many Italian families, we all moved into St. Vincent's Hospital for the duration. Before she died, we know she saw all her brothers and sisters who had gone before her, as well as her mother; we heard her talking to them. Having her family around her was always of utmost importance to her; now she had all her family (past and present) encircling her, and she left us peacefully. This was over fifteen years ago; I still miss her so much.

About six months after Mama died, I got a call to pick up my cat. My friend was moving to a new house and couldn't take Rogue with him. I was devastated. I couldn't bring that cat home; it was Alex's territory and there was no getting around it. There was no one else who could take him, and the thought of bringing him to a shelter (where I knew what happened to ten-year-old cats) was tearing me apart.

> One night, I dreamed I heard Mama shuffling outside my bedroom door. This was one of those dreams where everything is so real, you never realize you are dreaming. I heard her say, "Who'sa in my room?" like she had done so many times before. When she opened the door, she was carrying Rogue under her left arm. (She had never picked up either cat when she was alive.) I remember being so happy to see her, but very concerned because she had brought my cat into my

mother's house. "Mama!" I said, "It's so good to see you. But you can't bring him in here. Mom would never allow it." She just smiled and put Rogue in my arms. As she walked out the door, she said, "Nunju worry."

When I woke up, I told my mother about the dream. She thought about it for a while. Finally, she broke down and said we could give it a try—but if there were any fireworks, my cat would have to go. The next day I brought Rogue home. He and Alex eyed each other warily. I watched apprehensively as they circled each other, hissing, their ears pressed back tightly against their heads. After a minute or so, they seemed to lose interest in this territorial ritual. They just walked away from each other. After that, both cats coexisted peacefully with no further incident.

℘♦ℭ

When my father died in 1972, it was under unusual circumstances. My parents had recently divorced after nearly thirty years of marriage. My dad had remarried; shortly afterward he was diagnosed with inoperable melanoma. The night he died, my stepmother called me on the telephone and said, "Your father willed his body to science. Don't bother to come here because there will be no funeral." I was twenty-three years old, newly married myself, and I believed her. But it hurt.

Being deprived of a final good-bye was very hard for me to deal with. About a year later, I met a woman who had been at his funeral and was very surprised that she had not seen me there. This made me angry and resentful; it took many years before I could subconsciously accept my father's death. I never found his grave and could not put him to rest in my mind. Now and then, though, he makes an appearance in my dreams, just to let me know all is well and that he still loves me. My father was ravaged with cancer and turned white practically overnight from the chemotherapy. He died in his early fifties. But when he comes to me, he is the Daddy I knew as a child— young and robust, and tanned from the sun. He usually doesn't speak, but his expression is loving and his embrace is comforting. And I always awake from a dream of him with a warm, comfortable feeling that usually lasts throughout my day.

ℛ ✦ ℜ

Arlene M. from Thomaston shared a wonderful example of an Angelic visitation in the form of a dream visit from her grandfather.

I was very close to my grandfather. I was thirteen when he died and it broke my heart.

He had Parkinson's Disease, and toward the end of his life, he really didn't recognize us and couldn't distinguish between night and day. The day before he died, we had a family gathering. We always had our Thanksgiving dinners the Sunday before Thanksgiving so that my dad and uncle could hunt Thanksgiving Day.

Grandfather seemed so different. It seemed like he was relating to us by the look in his eyes and a smile on his face. He always used to tease me as a kid, and that day he tugged on a strand of my hair. I was surprised, because he hadn't been himself in months!

The next day, Grandfather died. Thinking it was morning, he got up out of bed and dressed himself with every button in place (Grandma always helped him before). She heard him get up and directed him back to bed because it was far from morning. Soon after, he took his last breath.

I always had feared death, and this was my first experience of losing someone close to me. I had so many questions. I felt numb all over. I wondered if he was experiencing peace.

A few nights later, I had a dream like no other. It seemed to answer all of my questions about my grandfather. I dreamed of walking through a country field of tall grass and following a path that led to a big old country home. It was the kind of home with a big welcoming front porch like the kind you'd see in the movies. I felt a force drawing me to this house. I eagerly went inside. It was bright and airy with big spacious rooms, and a big country kitchen that made me feel right at home. A huge staircase led up to an open loft on the upper level.

My grandfather always liked the country. He was a very practical, simple kind of man with a huge warm heart. In the center of the house was a massive fireplace with a huge fire burning. I was amazed by its warmth.

Then I looked up and noticed the door was opening. Just beyond the door, I saw a shadowy figure. It came out to greet me. It was Grandfather! I wanted to embrace him, but held back. I was afraid. Was he a ghost? He gently held me and said that everything was okay and gave me a warm smile. I commented on how beautiful and inviting this house was and on the fire in the fireplace. It burned so brightly. He told me he would always be there to help keep the fire burning.

When I woke up, I felt comforted. I felt that Grandfather was in Heaven, and that he would be my Guardian Angel who would always keep the fire burning. I knew I would never forget this dream.

∞✦∞

5th Degree Encounters: Physical Manifestations

There seems to be no end to the variety of manifestations Angels use when crossing into the physical realm. Whatever we need at the time, they can find in their celestial bag of tricks.

Tom Sprague of Bucks Harbor recalls an incident many years ago. As a child, he was uprooted from rural Maine when his family moved to a large city in southern Connecticut. Just living day-by-day in this alien environment was a terrifying prospect for a small child, used to the safety of small-town Maine.

> I think it is great that you are doing this book on Angels. I believe there are good Angels and bad Angels; therefore, I have never sought Angels as such. But when my family moved to Bridgeport, Connecticut, when I was eight, I had my first encounter with an Angel.

> All I had ever known before was the country. Now we lived in the downtown area of a very big city, and I was afraid of everything.

One day, my friends and I decided to go to a movie. The theater was several blocks from my home. When we got to the theater, I found myself alone. Somehow, I'd gotten separated from my friends. I became very frightened. I didn't know what to do, and had no idea how to get home—I couldn't remember where I lived! I was too afraid to do anything but stand there on the sidewalk, and I started to cry.

A strange man approached me and said, "Why are you crying, little boy?"

I was afraid of everything, but I didn't seem to be afraid of this stranger. I told him that I was lost, and I didn't know where I lived.

He simply said, "Walk with me."

And I did. I don't remember any conversation after that, but we walked and walked and walked until suddenly I spotted my house. I was so happy and yelled, "Thank you, mister!" as I ran home. I believe this man had to have been an Angel.

Anyone else would've looked for a policeman, but he just said, "Walk with me!"

ෂ♦ඥ

Here is a case where it seems the Angels enlisted the aid of a conveniently handy passerby to effect the rescue of children about to be swept out to sea. It comes, once again, from Everett Cross of Brewer.

Every summer, I visited Wood Island, where my mother was born. It is located in New Brunswick, Canada, twenty miles out to sea. The summer I was fifteen, I went with two island girls and one other boy to another island for a swim. This island was two miles away and had a nice sandy beach. We rowed in a boat called a dory.

While we were swimming, we didn't notice the fog coming in.

Within minutes, we couldn't see twenty feet in front of us. We jumped in the dory and headed for Wood Island. We rowed for hours till we were exhausted. We knew we were lost. The girls started praying. It was getting very late. Then we heard the sound of a motor. We shouted till we were hoarse, but couldn't be heard over the sound of the motor.

All of a sudden, the motor stopped.

We started shouting again—to our surprise, a man shouted back! He kept hollering until we could see his boat. We all climbed aboard his boat. He explained that his motor had stopped running for no reason at all. After we were all aboard, he turned on the switch, and the motor started right up. We knew right away that our prayers had been answered. He told us we had been headed out to sea; in fact, we were twenty miles from land!

ജ✦ര

There was another time in Everett Cross's life when Angels sent a stranger to help him. This happened in the late 1950s, while he was employed as a tree surgeon in Portland.

During the winter I had caught a bad case of sinus that caused my face to swell up so much that my eyes closed. My supervisor drove me to Mercy Hospital in Portland, where I was a patient for two weeks. At that time, my wife didn't drive, so she had to ride a bus to visit me in the hospital. On the bus one day, she began talking with another passenger and mentioned she was coming to visit me in the hospital. This woman carried a Bible; she said the Bible was her church and she would pray for me, which she did, at the hospital.

My doctor, Dr. Lappin, told me that X-rays showed a bone blocking the passage in the left side of my nose. The previous summer, I had been in a fist fight which I think caused the injury to my nose. I needed surgery to remove the blockage, and the doctor set up an appointment for the following Monday.

On Sunday, Mrs. Cook (the lady from the bus) visited me. She placed her hand on my head and nose and asked God to heal me.

The next day, I went to Dr. Lappin's office on Park Avenue in Portland to schedule surgery. He put a clamp on the left side of my nose, then said he must have the wrong side because he saw nothing there. He tried the right side. He told me then that my nose was clear of any blockage.

When I told him about Mrs. Cook, he said it must have been a miracle.

ℰ✦ℛ

D orothy Jordan of Warren had a vivid 5th Degree encounter; an excellent illustration of how Angels appear in the form most suited to their purpose.

Many years ago we lived in Walleston, Massachusetts, while my husband was attending college and I was the breadwinner in the family, when I had this remarkable experience.

I was working nights at the Boston Gear Works. I had to leave home each night about 10:00 p.m. and walk 1½ miles to where I boarded the streetcar to go the last several miles to work. I arrived home around 7:30 each morning. My young husband, Vernon, cared for our baby at night.

One morning when I reached home, Vernon asked, "Did you have anything strange happen to you last night? After you left, I had a great fear for you. I prayed. At the time you were to be at work (11:00 p.m.), the fear left me and I went to sleep. Anything strange happen?"

I answered, "Yes, very much so."

When I was about halfway from home to the streetcar, I heard someone behind me. I looked; a man was following me.

I began to run. He ran, also.

When he was almost to me, an enormous German Shepard dog appeared—*from nowhere*—and began to walk beside me. He wouldn't let the man anywhere near me. He growled, and the man following me knew the dog would attack him if he touched me.

That huge dog walked with me until I reached the streetcar safely.

As I boarded the streetcar, I looked back at the dog. The dog looked right back.

I knew this area well. I had never seen a dog like that there, and as I inquired of others from the neighborhood, they had never seen a dog like that, either.

I knew the Lord had answered my husband's prayer by sending His Angel in the form of a dog to protect me.

ℬ♦ℭ

Make no mistake: the Angels know what you need. They also know *when* you need it. This timing does not necessarily coincide with your own ideas of when you think you need it. An excellent case in point is the following story from Barbara Mooney Darling, of Wiscasset.

In 1992, I had a business on Route 1 in Edgecomb, in the old Edgecomb Post Office. I had been trying to sell that piece of property for eight years. I finally put my house up for sale, as well, and that had been on the market for three years.

One day as I was leaving the shop, a man pulled up in an old, dark green car. He asked if it was all right to park there. I said, "Sure, but why?"

He answered, "Well, I'd like to pray behind your building."

This struck me as rather unusual, but he did seem reasonably harmless. He was an ordinary looking fellow, dressed in a white shirt and dark pants. His long, dark hair was pulled back in a ponytail.

I thought about his request for a moment, then answered him with a question of my own.

"Well, as long as you're going to pray," I asked, "would you say a prayer for me that I can sell this building?" He said he surely would.

With that, he walked to the side of the building, crossed his hands on his chest, and stood there facing east as I pulled away. Now, I'm normally very cautious, and I was amazed at myself for leaving the premises with a stranger there. I knew right away that it was something more than just a man who wanted to pray. But on the way home, something said to me, *"You can't go back and check on him. You've got to accept this on faith."* I can't say for sure that I heard a voice, but I was very aware of this thought. So I didn't go back; but when I got home, I did call two friends of mine to tell them what had happened—just in case something came from it, I'd have some proof.

The next morning, I got a call from the real estate broker who had the place for sale. He said he had an offer to purchase the building. And by the end of the week, I had two more offers. I not only sold that property, I sold my house, as well.

The funny thing is, if I'd sold my properties any earlier, I would not have found the house I'm living in now, which is absolutely perfect for me!

℘✦℃

Guardian Angels seem to do their best work when you're in danger. There is another type of physical manifestation where the Angel must act so quickly, it doesn't bother to take on any physical form, yet manages to make physical contact to accomplish its mission. One such encounter happened to Jean S. of Rockland, some years ago while a resident of Crozet, Virginia.

I had been working the night shift and was driving home at about 7:30 a.m. On my way home, I had to make a turn at a railroad overpass. I was so tired, it was a struggle just to keep my eyes open. Fatigue finally conquered me, and I fell asleep at the wheel.

Something hit me in the head and woke me up—at the precise moment I should have been making that turn at the railroad bridge. My hands were still on the steering wheel, but before I could react, the wheel jerked by itself and made the turn for me.

I firmly believe that I had an Angel watching over me so I wouldn't crash into that overpass. I've never had any reason to suspect it was anything different.

℘ ✦ ℆

Afterword

As *Angel Country* went to press, a flurry of new correspondence came my way. Too late for inclusion in this volume, these stories cry out to be told. I expect that I will continue to hear from people eager to share their experiences with others, and I welcome the input.

Sophy Burnham's book, *A Book of Angels*, was certainly not the first popular book about Angels. But its personal approach—the sharing of individual encounters with Angelic beings, has broken down the barriers for countless ordinary human beings to share their Angelic Encounters with others.

Burnham told Newsweek magazine, "My book gave people permission to say, 'Yes, this happened to me, too.' "

For every encounter I have related in *Angel Country*, there are hundreds more waiting to be told.

If this book has touched you in any way, if it has enabled you to recollect an experience with a messenger from God that might enrich another's life, I would like to hear from you.

You can reach me by mail, FAX, telephone, E-Mail, or even on the World Wide Web (Internet).

Please write me at the following address:

Angelis Press
P.O. Box 1018
Rockland, ME 04841-1018

You may also FAX your letter to (207) 596-5650.

If you prefer to record your story, I maintain a 24-hour answering machine at the same number.

E-Mail Address: angels@midcoast.com

WEB Site: http://www.midcoast.com/~angels/

Additional copies of *Angel Country* are available by mail. For your convenience, an order form can be found on the last page.

80♦03

$\mathcal{R}$esources &

$\mathcal{R}$ecommended $\mathcal{R}$eading

Adler, Mortimer J.   *The Angels and Us*
                             MacMillan, Inc., New York 1982

Burnham, Sophy   *A Book of Angels*
                             Ballantine Books, New York 1989

                         Angel Letters
                             Ballantine Books, New York 1991

Chessman, Harriet S.   *Literary Angels*
                             Ballantine Books, New York 1994

Church, F. Forrester   *Entertaining Angels: A Guide for
                         Atheists and True Believers*
                             Harper & Row, San Francisco 1987

Davidson, Gustav   *A Dictionary of Angels*
                             Free Press, New York 1980

Daniel, Alma   *Ask Your Angels*
Wyllie, Timothy &   Ballantine Books, New York 1992
Ramer, Andrew

Gallup, Alec
& Gallup, George, Jr.

Teen Belief in Angels Is on the Rise.
Princeton, NJ: Gallup Poll 1988

Gallup, George

*A Surprising Number of Americans
Believe in Paranormal Phenomena*
Princeton, NJ: Gallup Poll 1978

Graham, Billy

Angels, God's Secret Agents
Doubleday 1975/ Random 1986/
Word, Inc. 1994

Humann, Harvey

The Many Faces of Angels
DeVorss & Co., Marina Del Rey,
California 1986

Joppie, A.S.

All About Angels
Baker Book House
Grand Rapids, Michigan 1973

Jung, Carl G.

*The Interpretation of Nature and the
Psyche. Synchronicity: An Acausal
Connecting Principle*
Pantheon Books, New York 1955

Newsweek Magazine

*Angels: America's Latest Search for
Spiritual Meaning Has A Halo Effect.*
December 27, 1993

Random House

An Angel A Week
Ballantine Books, New York 1992

Steiger, Brad

Guardian Angels & Spirit Guides
Penguin Books, New York 1995

TIME Magazine

The New Age of Angels
December 27, 1993

Taylor, Terry Lynn

*Messengers of Light:The Angels Guide
to Spiritual Growth*
H.J. Kramer, Tiburon, California 1990

Urantia Foundation

The Urantia Book
Chicago, Illinois 1955

To order additional copies of *Angel Country*, complete the information below:

Ship to: (please print)

_____
Name

_____
Address:

_____
City, State, Zip

_____ Copies of *Angel Country* @ $7.95 each $ _____

Maine residents add 6% tax $ _____

Postage & handling @ $2.50 per book $ _____

Total Amount of Order $ _____

Make check or money order payable to *Angel Country*

or

Charge my

 ☐    ☐

Date: ____ / ____ / ____

Account No. ____ ____ ____ ____

Expiration Date: ____ / ____

Signature: _____

Send to: *Angelis Press* ● P.O. Box 1018 ● Rockland, ME 04841